Introduction

The landscapes around Cambridge are beautiful. With fens to the east, gentle hills to the west, colourful towns and thatched cottages, these walks form an extraordinarily varied 84-mile circular route around the city, through rural Cambridgeshire, picturesque North Essex and Hertfordshire.

This book is a celebration of these landscapes. It is also a guide to the northern half of a long-distance path called the Harcamlow Way. Fred Matthews and Harry Bitten originally devised it as a figure-of-eight walk in the 1970s. As the name hints, the Harcamlow runs from Harlow to Cambridge and back again. My guide to the southern half (through Herts and Essex) was published in 2014.

Ordnance Survey explorer maps of Cambridge (209), Saffron Walden (195) and Bishop's Stortford (194) will be very useful. There are no dedicated Harcamlow waymarks, but the walks are on public lanes or paths and there are nearly always signs or arrows of some sort. Occasionally, I've suggested alternatives to the original route, mainly to give better public transport options. Buses and pubs change over time, but I've listed the current ones as starting points. It's worth checking ahead if you're relying on stopping somewhere for refreshments or catching a train.

Besides a number of picturesque country pubs, this lovely northern loop of the Harcamlow Way passes windmills and watermills, landscaped gardens and wild woodland, fields of poppies or glades of snowdrops, medieval churches and state-of-the-art science centres. There are ancient monuments, like Saxon Fleam Dyke or the huge Roman burial mounds at Bartlow. The walks pass stately homes with beautiful gardens at Anglesey Abbey, Audley End and Wimpole Hall, and dozens of delightful villages.

This is a route that will please both hardened hikers and afternoon strollers. A really energetic walker might complete the whole circuit in four days, while, by using the transport suggestions to shorten the sections, others could happily divide it into eighteen or more leisurely excursions. Happy walking!

Phoebe Taplin, 2015

Cambridge to Waterbeach

8 miles

Into the busy, historic centre of the city and out again along the winding river.

From Cambridge railway station, walk straight ahead and turn right, opposite **Botanic Garden (1)**, onto Hills Road, leading into the middle of Cambridge. Keep going in this direction for more than a mile, following Regent Street, St Andrew's Street and forking left onto Sidney Street, all lined with interesting buildings. Go on along Bridge Street, past **Round Church (2)**, onto Magdalene Street.

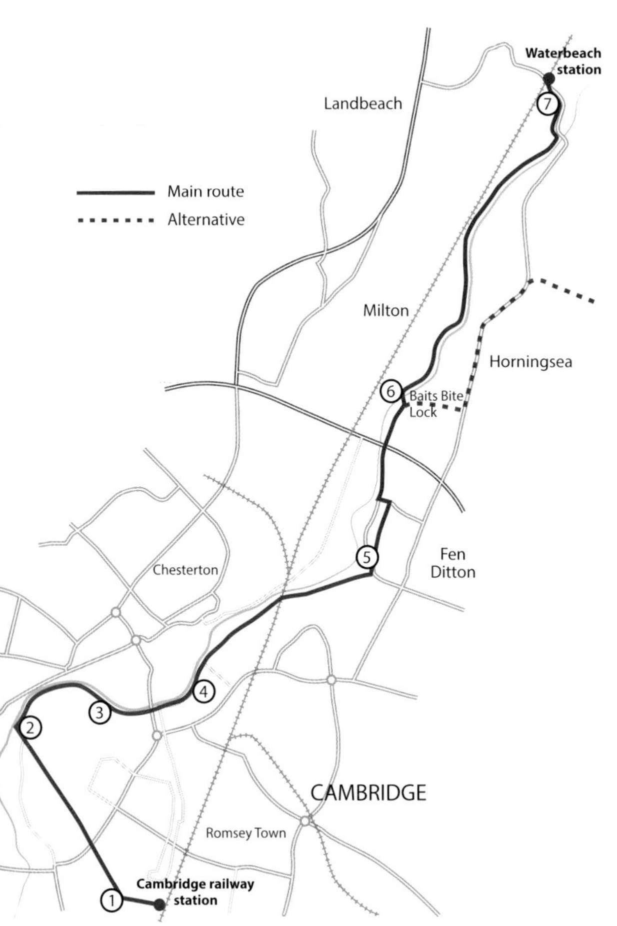

Just before **River Cam (3)**, turn right onto waterside path and keep following it for nearly two miles, past parks and boathouses. Eventually, a little road leads you past the tall, brick chimney of **Cambridge Museum of Technology (4)**.

Keeping water on left, follow tarmac path ahead through meadows. Soon after going under the railway, leave cycle route 51 and take grassy path straight over footbridge, towards church tower in **Fen Ditton (5)**. Near village, go right through a gap in hedge, then left to find a gate and follow lane beyond, past St Mary's church.

Take a sharp left at war memorial onto Church Street, past King's Head pub. As the road swings left and becomes Green End, take path straight across recreation ground and along field edge. (Or stay on Green End for the Plough pub.) Turn left at end of path along track between hedges and right along a tree-lined lane. Take signed footpath towards Horningsea.

After passing underneath the A14, follow gravel path through trees to reach a cottage by **Baits Bite Lock (6)**. At this point you have a choice: for the station, cross footbridges at lock and keep going along the river towards Waterbeach. After two miles, turn left at bridge and follow footpath beside road, past **Cow Hollow Wood (7)**, to reach Waterbeach railway station.

Alternatively, you could follow the original Harcamlow route for a longer walk: turn right at **(6)** across fields and left on road through Horningsea. Take second path right after the village, signposted Quy and Lode. Here, pick up directions from third paragraph of next walk.

Above left: View from Magdelene Bridge.
Above centre: Round Church.
Above right: Cam-side path.

LOOK OUT FOR: Cambridge University's beautiful **Botanic Garden** **(1)** encompasses 40 acres of varied plant life and landscapes (www.botanic.cam.ac.uk, open daily, £5).

Cambridge is one of the most interesting and historic cities in the world. Among many ancient buildings, the 12th-century **Round Church** or **Church of the Holy Sepulchre** **(2)** is especially unusual.

The **River Cam** **(3)** is central to local life. In the city you will see numerous punts; and there are always rowing boats training for races on the stretch up to Fen Ditton, where the church has a weathervane shaped like a rowing boat.

Cambridge Museum of Technology **(4)** is housed in a 19th-century sewage pumping station. This volunteer-run museum was created to preserve and restore the original, steam-powered machinery (www.museumoftechnology.com, open Sunday afternoons, £3.50).

There has been a settlement at **Fen Ditton** **(5)** since the late Stone Age. It was an important medieval trading post on the Cam with a 12th-century church. You cross the remains of medieval wharfs as you enter the village.

FOOD AND DRINK: Central Cambridge has lots of pubs and cafés. The walk passes the **Fort St George** on Midsummer Common after a couple miles, the **King's Head** and the **Plough** in Fen Ditton (www.theploughfenditton.co.uk), and the **Bridge** near Waterbeach.

TRANSPORT: There are hourly trains from **Waterbeach** back to Cambridge. For people looking to shorten the walk, there are buses at **Chesterton**, over the river from the **Museum of Technology** **(4)**. For those wanting to walk further, you can go via **Horningsea** to reach buses at **Lode** or walk back from **(6)** along far side of river.

Below left: Cam in winter.
Below centre: Cam-side path.
Below right: Fort St George pub.

Waterbeach to Fulbourn

10 miles

A lovely cross-country ramble through fenland, along reed-lined rivers, and past the gardens of Anglesey Abbey.

From Waterbeach station head away from the village, past car park, and take path that runs parallel to road, ignoring all turnings, until you reach the River Cam at **Clayhithe** **(1)**. Turn left onto road, right across a bridge, ignore the towpath, and take next left turn along tarmac lane. Turn right through a farmyard and go on along path beyond.

After about 100m, turn right at yellow arrow. Walk straight across the field and along grassy path. As you draw level with Eye Hall Farm on the right, look out for 'Fen Rivers' waymark (with eel logo) and follow it diagonally right through paddocks and gate. Go straight on through fields to track near village of **Horningsea** **(2)** and turn left along bridleway signposted to Quy and Lode.

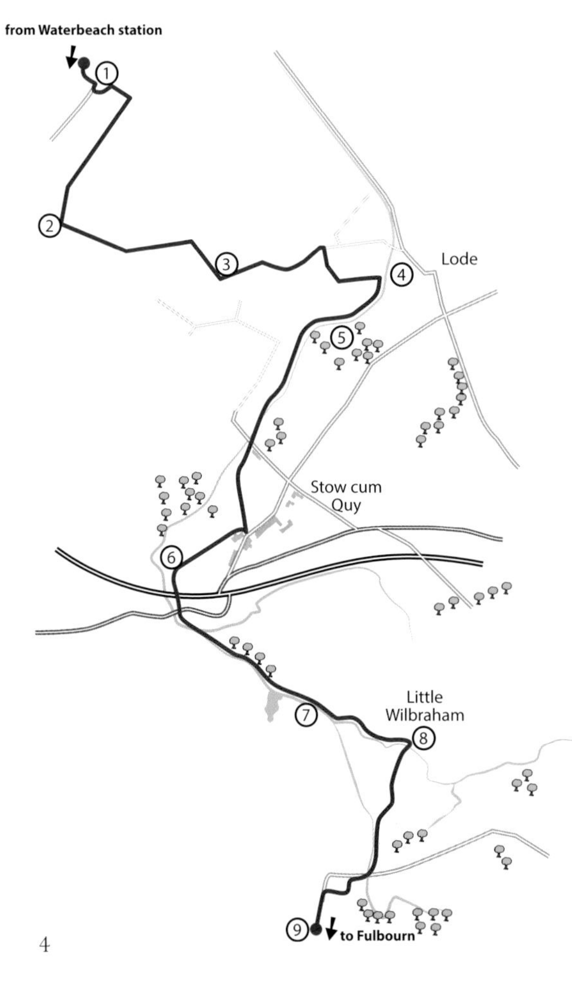

Follow this track for a mile, ignoring all turnings, until it passes under two rows of pylons and over a ditch. Next to a green sign introducing **Quy Fen** **(3)**, turn right through metal gate and keep left through bushes and trees until you come to long, narrow lake lined with reeds. Walk along right-hand edge of it.

At far end, turn briefly left and then follow the fence right to find metal gate. Go through gate and walk diagonally right across field to reach another gate in far corner and a footbridge with a sign to Lode. Cross bridge and follow path beyond, around the right-hand edge of another narrow lake. Follow waymarked path slightly left across open country towards a line of conifers. Carry on along grassy track and take first waymarked turning on right.

At T-junction, turn left along another track and then right into woods. Take first left turn through woods, following path out of trees again and along edge of field, towards **Lode Mill** **(4)**. Turn right along near side of Quy Water and follow this path for two miles. (Alternatively, for Lode buses, café and entrance to the National Trust's Anglesey Abbey, go straight on past the mill and right.)

Walking along Quy Water, past stone bridge and buildings, you catch glimpses on the far bank of the National Trust (NT) gardens of **Anglesey Abbey** **(5)**. The riverside path goes on through open fields, drained centuries ago so farmers could work the land.

Above left: Anglesey Abbey.
Above centre: Quy Fen in winter.
Above right: Lode Mill.

Reaching a lane, turn left over bridge and on for 50m, then right near bench onto footpath along left side of fields. At a band of trees, head left through two kissing gates and between trees along a path that becomes a track.

At end of track, turn right along Orchard Street (Wheatsheaf pub is left). Turn right again onto footpath. Keep left on track and left again on path across fields. Go through gate and turn left along the drive of Quy Mill Hotel **(6)** to find tunnel under the A14.

Go on along tarmac path beyond, cross and turn right along busy road. Go over bridge and then left along Little Wilbraham River **(7)**. Follow riverside path (sometimes a bit overgrown in places) with rush-filled waterway on left, ignoring all turnings.

After nearly two miles, cross wooden footbridge and follow grassy path ahead. Walk on past private fishing pond, through trees and along edge of field. Follow path right past the gate of Hawk Mill Farm **(8)**. Take waymarked path slightly left along field edge, with tall hedge on right, and then diagonally right across fields towards distant silo. Cross footbridge and follow grassy track beside ditch beyond left to a road.

Turn right along road and left onto footpath across fields, then right along fenced path around silo to enter Fulbourn **(9)**. Turn left along Station Road, over railway, and follow road until it turns right. The Harcamlow Way continues along path to left, but for pubs and buses turn right here past St Vigor's church.

LOOK OUT FOR: There has been an inn by the bridge at Clayhithe **(1)** since medieval times, including the Jack and Eel pub recorded here in 1765. Near house with decorative gables is the Conservators of the River Cam HQ. The conservators were first appointed in 1702 to make the 'River Cham … more navigable from Clay-Hithe Ferry, to the Queen's Mill'.

Quy Fen **(3)** was historically common land, shared between local parishes. Villagers were allowed to cut peat and catch fish, but not to graze animals. The lakes and mounds are remnants of the Victorian coprolite industry, which involved digging up phosphatised clay nodules to use as fertiliser. Quy is pronounced to rhyme with 'why' and originally meant 'Cow Island'.

Lode Mill **(4)** is a working watermill that produces stoneground flour, and there has been a mill here since at least 1086 as it is listed in Domesday Book. Quy Water is an artificial waterway, now higher than the surrounding land.

Right: Moorhen on Quy water.

Above left: Quy Water in summer.
Above centre: Path near Little Wilbraham.
Above right: Riverside path near Anglesey Abbey.

Anglesey Abbey **(5)**, beyond the mill, was once a medieval priory, but today's house and grand gardens were created by 20th-century philanthropist Lord Fairhaven, who left them to the National Trust when he died in 1966 (www.nationaltrust.org.uk/anglesey-abbey).

Quy Mill Hotel **(6)**, which also features in Domesday Book, was rebuilt in the 19th century, when the mill was a thriving business, producing bread until after the Second World War.

The area around the Little Wilbraham River **(7)** is one of the few remaining areas of fenland near Cambridge. It forms the southern edge of what was once nearly 100 miles of marshes, stretching to Lincoln. Most of the land has now been reclaimed for farming.

Fulbourn **(9)** was once a staging post between Cambridge and Newmarket, boasting more than 20 coaching inns. The Six Bells on the High Street is one of three surviving pubs and dates from the 15th century.

FOOD AND DRINK: Between the Bridge at Clayhithe (Chef and Brewer; 'classic pub food') and well-supplied Fulbourn, the most convenient stops are the Wheatsheaf pub or fancy Quy Mill Hotel **(6)** (www.cambridgequymill.co.uk at Stow-cum-Quy). The old mill is pricey, but idyllic and perfectly located for a just-over-halfway break. A detour off the route from **(4)** brings you to the NT café in Anglesey Abbey and entrance to the picturesque gardens.

TRANSPORT: Waterbeach has hourly trains to Cambridge. Citibuses 1 and 3 run regularly from opposite the Six Bells in Fulbourn to Cambridge bus and train stations. Lode has an hourly bus (number 10) to Cambridge bus station if you want to divide the route.

Left: Lodge house at Clayhithe.

Fulbourn to Horseheath

10 miles

The wide-open fields and ancient earthworks of this section make a great contrast with the previous walk's rivers and marshes.

From Fulbourn High Street, follow Church Lane right past almshouses. At corner of Station Road, take signed footpath straight on towards Fulbourn Fen (**1**) and keep going in this direction. Turn right at wooden signpost along gravel bridleway, then left along tarmac lane and left again following signs for Fleam Dyke.

Keep on along path between fence and trees, over bridge and straight, then curving right beside a stream.

Turn left onto mud track and right towards Fleam Dyke (**2**). Climb steps and walk along path on top with good views of land around.

Pass a brick pumping station and, after one and a half miles, Mutlow Hill (**3**), a Bronze Age burial mound. Path goes through trees and over A11 on footbridge. Carry on, with trees crowning Fleam Dyke, passing flint buildings of Durngate Farm after a mile.

The path eventually descends to ground level, but continues clearly ahead along edge of field next to turbines of Wadlow Wind Farm (**4**). Soon after wind farm, turn right along a defined track for 500m and left at signpost, along field edge and ditch.

Follow path right then diagonally left, across sports field, into Balsham (**5**). Walk past church, turn right along Church Lane and left onto High Street past post office.

Fulbourn
Mutlow Hill
Bedford Gap
Balsham
Horseheath

Above: Fulbourn Fen.

Above left: Fleam Dyke.
Above centre: Steps up to Fleam Dyke.
Above right: Horseheath.

Turn right just before butcher's shop along little Woodhall Lane, following axe waymarks for **Icknield Way** **(6)**. Keep straight along this track for half a mile, turn left beyond Wood Hall and right shortly after for nearly a mile. Turn left along **Roman Road** **(7)**, leaving Icknield Way, and keep straight along this grassy track for nearly two miles, crossing road and footbridge.

Eventually, opposite metal gate at foot of slope, a broad, grassy path beside a ditch leads right, winding through fields towards **Horseheath** **(8)**. Follow this path over bridge, through kissing gate and along edge of fields to emerge into a Horseheath cul-de-sac. Turn briefly right, left on Audley Way, right past village green, and right again to reach bus stop and Old Red Lion pub.

LOOK OUT FOR: **Fulbourn Fen** **(1)** became a nature reserve in 1967 and is a Site of Special Scientific Interest (SSSI), managed by the Wildlife Trusts. There are wonderful snowdrops in the early spring woods. You can take an alternative route through the reserve, following the map at the entrance.

Fleam Dyke **(2)** is another SSSI and also an archaeological scheduled monument. This ancient bank, possibly dating back to the Iron Age, was a defensive barrier between warring 6th-century Saxon tribes.

Four thousand-year-old **Mutlow Hill** **(3)** is a Bronze Age burial mound. Romans later used the site for a temple. A signboard nearby has lots more information.

Completed in 2012, the 13 turbines of **Wadlow Wind Farm** **(4)** can generate enough renewable electricity to power nearly 17,000 homes.

Describing itself as the 'oldest road in Britain', the **Icknield Way** **(6)** is the basis of another great, long-distance path. It joins the Ridgeway in Buckinghamshire and the Peddars Way in Norfolk to form a prehistoric route from Dorset to the East Coast.

The **Roman Road** **(7)**, along a chalk ridge, was once known as Woolstreet Way, suggesting Norfolk yarn traders used it.

FOOD AND DRINK: The thatched Black Bull pub just beyond the butcher's in **Balsham** **(5)** is a great place for a lunch stop (blackbull-balsham.co.uk), and the Old Red Lion in **Horseheath** **(8)** is a welcoming destination (www.theoldredlion.co.uk).

TRANSPORT: Citibuses 1 and 3 run regularly from Cambridge to **Fulbourn** and bus 13 goes every half an hour back from **Horseheath**. You could divide the route at **Balsham** (change at Linton for bus 13 to Cambridge).

Left: Balsham church with close-up of face on the brickwork.

Horseheath to Saffron Walden

11 miles

Walk through Roman burial mounds at Bartlow Hills, a string of pretty villages and the colourful town of Saffron Walden.

From the **Old Red Lion pub** (**1**), turn right and follow Linton Road and Haverhill Road. Turn right at signpost through metal gate and along edge of cricket pitch. Cross footbridge and take path beyond, across the A1307.

Continue on far side along edge of field with views opening up ahead. Walk through gap in hedge and turn left onto grassy track, following the sometimes-muddy way through corner of field onto a sunken, tree-lined path.

Turn right onto path and continue in this direction for two miles, past woods and fields, crossing gravel track. Finally, turn right for three-quarters of a mile along road into Bartlow. Turn left through churchyard and head left of **Bartlow church** (**2**) to find a fenced path, which crosses River Granta and disused railway, and emerges by large Roman burial mounds.

Turn right through **Bartlow Hills** (**3**) and follow another fenced path through trees. Just before road, turn left onto path parallel to road. Turn left onto lane

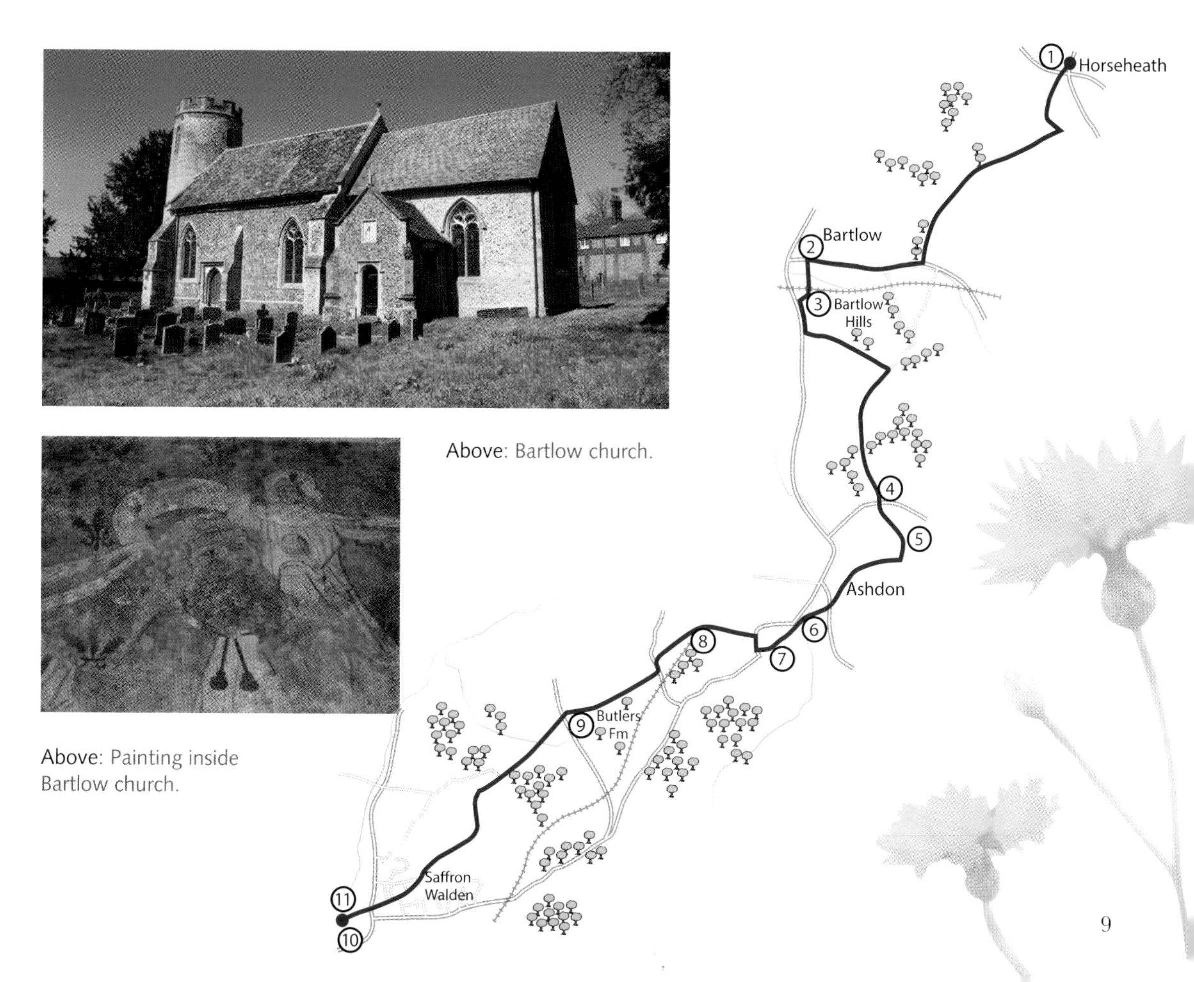

Above: Bartlow church.

Above: Painting inside Bartlow church.

Above left: Bartlow Hills.
Above centre: Steventon End.
Above right: Bragg's Mill.

at end, past round brick tower, and left again onto track for half a mile past trees.

Where the track swings left towards a private sign, turn right downhill and keep going in this direction, keeping hedge (where it exists) on left. At junction of tracks, keep going straight on along lane through beech trees. Follow this track past lovely parkland and picturesque houses of **Steventon End** **(4)**.

Cross a road and stile and carry on uphill along edge of paddock. Go over another stile, follow footpath ahead and cross lane to **Bragg's Mill** **(5)**. Beyond the windmill, head right on lane and take path at end between cottage and shed, along tree tunnel.

At gap in trees, follow waymark right along field edge, with hedge on right. At corner of field, go straight through gap and on, following path (with hedge still on right) as it winds downhill. At junction of waymarked paths, keep left to reach lane and turn right along it. Cross Radwinter Road and keep straight on far side beside half-timbered house. Head diagonally left across field beyond and follow path to emerge by footbridge behind **Ashdon Village Museum** **(6)**.

Cross bridge and turn immediately left, taking path that climbs through field, turning right at top. Fork left on grassy track, with **All Saints' church** **(7)** soon visible to the right, and turn right to cross stile. Turn right again between Guildhall and cottage into churchyard. Turn left out of gate, cross road and turn right beside brick houses. Turn left along Fallowden Lane and follow it out of village.

Keep going past farm and straight on along bridleway, turning left behind **Halt Cottage** **(8)** and right past Springmead. Follow well-defined bridleway and turn left along lane at end.

Turn right at Muntjac Nurseries, through metal gates and past greenhouses, to reach waymarked path beyond. Keep going the same way for three-quarters of a mile along grassy track to **Butlers Farm** **(9)**.

Follow track right, round farm buildings, and continue on far side in same direction. Follow as track winds through fields to wood called Long Grove. Turn right beside trees on track to corner of wood and then go straight on along path through field ahead.

On far side of field, turn left along track, then right along line of trees. You will soon see the spire of **St Mary's church** **(10)** ahead. Keep walking towards it. The track becomes a suburban road (Sheds Lane), then Pound Walk, and eventually reaches colourful Castle Street, with lovely **Bridge End Gardens** **(11)** to the right. At end of the road, turn left towards High Street for pubs and buses.

Left: Halt Cottage, Ashdon.

Above left: Ashdon.
Above centre: Castle Street, Saffron Walden.
Above right: Rose and Crown, Ashdon.

LOOK OUT FOR: The wonderful Norman tower of **Bartlow church** (**2**) is one of only two round towers in Cambridgeshire. Inside, fragments of a wall painting survive from the 15th century, including the top half of St Christopher with the Christ child on his shoulder, and a lonely dragon, minus his St George.

Bartlow Hills (**3**) are a series of huge barrows, the largest surviving Roman burial mounds in western Europe. The hills are made of soil and chalk in layers and the tallest hill (with steps) is 15m high. Inside the mounds, 19th-century archaeologists found brick chambers, once lit by iron lamps, with the cremated remains of the dead and objects from the 1st and 2nd centuries AD.

William Haylock, a carpenter from Ashdon, built **Bragg's Mill** (**5**) in 1757 (www.ashdonwindmilltrust.co.uk).

Ashdon Village Museum (**6**) is a fabulous nostalgic labyrinth of old rural artefacts and forgotten Victoriana. Open Wednesday and Sunday afternoons in summer, its retro music and homemade cakes are worth stopping for (www.ashdonvillagemuseum.co.uk, free entry).

The area around **All Saints' church** (**7**) is the site of Ashdon's original medieval village, represented now by a few cottages and the timber-framed Guildhall. Much of the church itself dates from the 14th century with high round windows, fragments of stained glass and a beamed roof.

The steam train-themed nameplate and weather vane on **Halt Cottage** (**8**) and the sunken track nearby are reminders of a disused railway. Work on the Saffron Walden branch line began in 1863, but it was closed a century later by Dr Beeching. The old line runs on through nearby **Shadwell Wood**, an area of ancient woodland with a carpet of wild garlic in spring. It is now a nature reserve managed by the Essex Wildlife Trust.

Early 17th-century **Butlers Farm** (**9**) was probably built by Thomas Howard, Earl of Suffolk, Lord Treasurer to King James I.

St Mary's church (**10**), with its 60m-high spire, is the largest parish church in Essex. Have a look inside at the stained glass and the angelic Trompeta Real pipes by the organ.

The restored Victorian **Bridge End Gardens** (**11**) boasts an art gallery, yew-hedge maze, walled kitchen garden and sloping lawns with a hexagonal summerhouse.

FOOD AND DRINK: The cakes in **Ashdon Village Museum**'s little teashop are so good that it's worth planning the walk on a Wednesday or Sunday just to eat them! The **Three Hills** in Bartlow and the **Rose and Crown** in Ashdon are both very close to (but not quite on) the route and make great stopping points. Saffron Walden is packed with bars, cafés and hotels. The first pub you pass is the unpretentious **Victory** on Little Walden Road.

TRANSPORT: Stagecoach bus 13 runs from Cambridge to **Horseheath**. There are numerous buses from **Saffron Walden** to Bishop's Stortford, Cambridge and elsewhere. Audley End railway station (trains to London and Cambridge) is nearby. **Ashdon** (bus 59 to Saffron Walden) is a good place to break this section into two shorter walks.

Saffron Walden to Newport

6 miles

This rewarding walk includes the chance to explore historic Audley End.

Turn off High Street in **Saffron Walden** **(1)** onto Abbey Lane, past United Reformed church. At end of road, go through metal gate into landscaped **Audley Park** **(2)** and take path slightly left with tall trees along it and views right towards Temple of Victory across the valley. Keep straight in this direction to emerge through another gate onto Audley End Road.

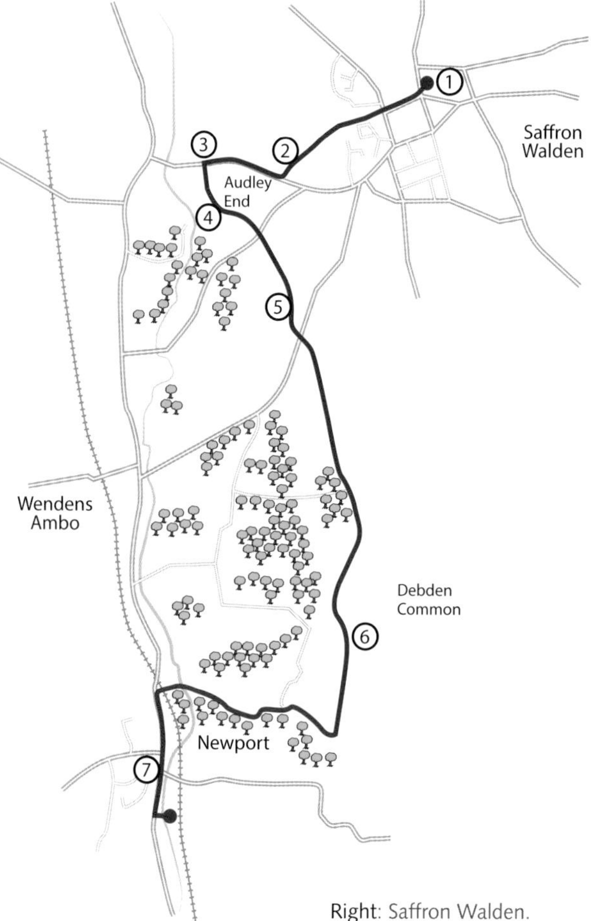

Turn right along side of road until a white signpost points left to 'College of St Mark'. (The main gate for **Audley End** **(3)** is a little further.) Turn left along a lane between rows of whitewashed, 18th-century cottages. Turn left through a gate that says 'Private: Donrobin Farms. Abbey Farm' (it is a public path) and follow this lane as it winds past **St Mark's College** **(4)** and farm buildings to road.

Cross over road and follow track ahead. About 50m beyond the power lines turn right over a stream and immediately left on wooded path called **Beechy Ride** **(5)**. Keep stream on left as path climbs up little slope to busy B1052. Cross and walk on through trees, with stream still on left, then along right-hand edge of field into more trees.

Turn left over footbridge and right along edge of wood. Follow path, keeping trees on right. Turn right over another bridge and take path beyond, between a fence and trees. Cross third footbridge and continue straight up right-hand edge of field. At corner of field, turn left, with hedge on right, and follow waymarked path around edge of wood, **Rosy Grove** **(6)**, and down right-hand edge of a large field.

Right: Saffron Walden.

Above left: Audley End.
Above centre: Beechy Ride.
Above right: Newport High Street.

Go on through little tree tunnel and downhill. At foot of hill, turn right along wooded path beside stream (overlapping very briefly with Harcamlow Book 1). Walk past a footbridge and keep on through trees and along the track. When the trees end, continue in same general direction with glimpses ahead of Newport's distant church.

The grassy path eventually becomes a lane and leads under the railway to main road. Turn left along Belmont Hill and Newport's picturesque **High Street (7)**. After about half a mile, turn left again onto Station Road.

LOOK OUT FOR: The medieval wealth and name of **Saffron Walden (1)** came from local crocus-growing to produce saffron. A trundle round the town trail (www.visitsaffronwalden.gov.uk/pdf/Saffron-Walden-Town-Trail.pdf) is a great way to start, passing medieval shops, half-timbered inns, the Georgian town hall, and the ruins of a 12th-century castle tucked behind the brick museum.

Much of the current interior of English Heritage-owned **Audley End (3)** pays ornate homage to the mansion's past as one of England's grandest Jacobean houses. When Henry VIII dissolved Walden Abbey, his Chancellor, Lord Audley, converted the buildings. Audley's grandson Thomas Howard rebuilt it on a palatial scale to entertain James I. 'Capability' Brown remodelled the lovely gardens in the 18th century (www.english-heritage.org.uk, £16; gardens-only in winter, £10).

The area around **St Mark's College (4)** was once a medieval village called Brookwalden, which served Walden Abbey. The oldest parts of the college, now a residential youth centre, date from the 13th century and were a hospital for Benedictine monks (www.stmarkscollege.co.uk).

The High Street in **Newport** is lined with mansions and old cottages, including the late 15th-century Monk's Barn. The upper storey has an oriel window with a sill carved to show Mary and Jesus, flanked by angels.

FOOD AND DRINK: **Saffron Walden** and **Newport** both have a good choice of refreshments, and there is a café inside **Audley End (3)**. Otherwise, there is nothing en route except some lovely picnic places.

TRANSPORT: **Saffron Walden**'s train station is beyond **Audley End**, but buses and taxis connect it with the town. Buses run every hour from Cambridge. Hourly bus 301 connects Bishop's Stortford, Newport, Audley End and Saffron Walden. **Newport** is also on the London (Liverpool Street) to Cambridge railway.

Right: A Newport window.

Newport to Chrishall

9 miles

Rolling hills, woods, fields and farms on a delightful walk between thatched villages.

From Newport railway station, walk along Station Road and turn right onto High Street. Soon after Indian restaurant, turn left towards **St Mary's church** (**1**). Walk through churchyard and right along path just beyond church. Take permissive path diagonally left after tennis courts, through gate and along Tenterfields Road.

Turn right and immediately left along lane with cottages. Keep straight up gravel track to go under M11 and bear right beyond motorway along track past clumps of trees. Just before pylons, turn sharp left uphill, then right at top and under pylons. Continue for a mile in this general direction along grassy tracks and finally a lane down into **Arkesden** (**2**). Turn right and right again through village, passing a pub.

Follow lane out of village, ignoring right turn to church and footpath on left. Turn left along a driveway to **Chardwell Farm** (**3**). Immediately before gate at end, turn right on path and follow fences and hedges uphill, turning right along a line of poplars, which becomes a hedge. Turn left at next field boundary. When hedge swings left, go straight on down field towards trees. (If field is impassable, walk round edge.)

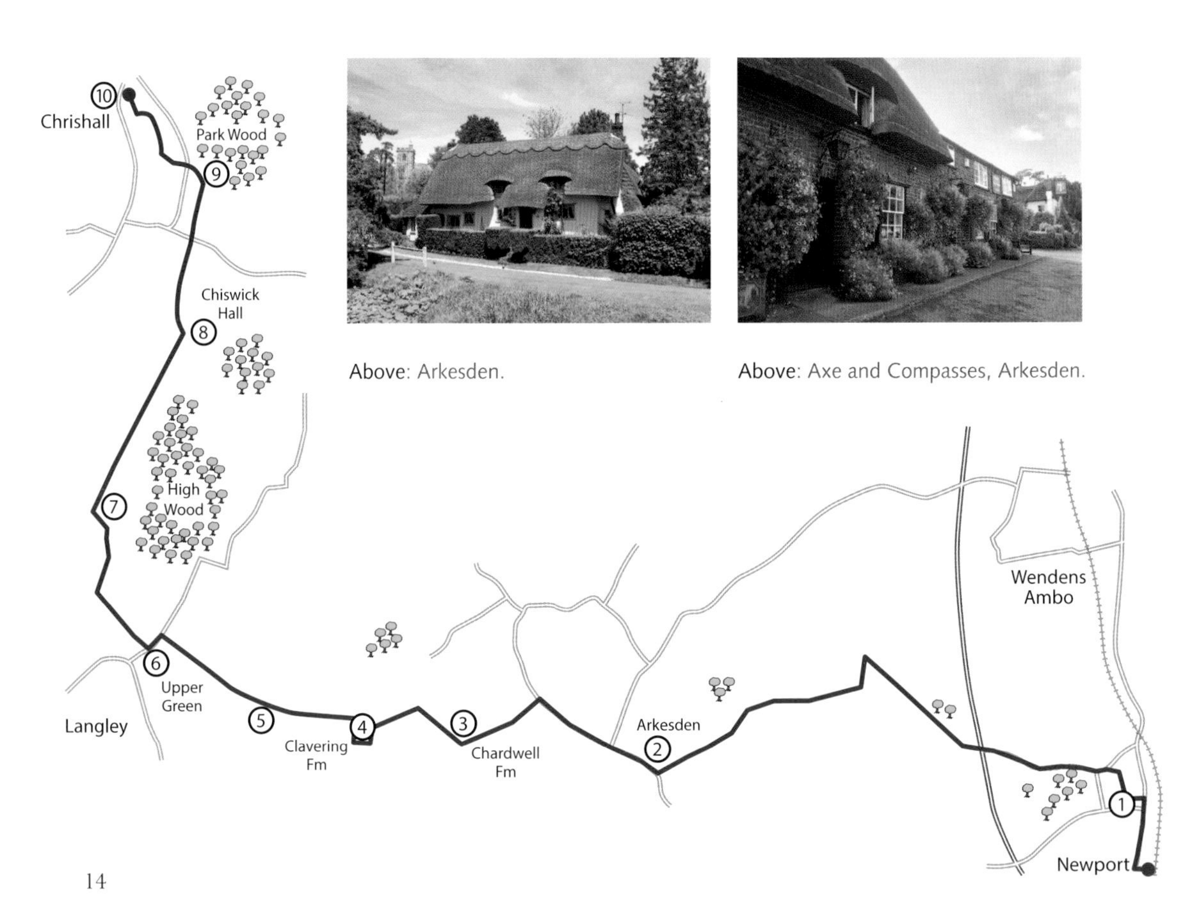

Above: Arkesden.

Above: Axe and Compasses, Arkesden.

Above left: Newport High Street.
Above centre: Stile near Clavering Farm.
Above right: Path between Newport and Arkesden.

Go down wooden steps in trees and over stile. Turn left towards orchard, over another stile, across footbridge and along little wooded path beside the **pond at Clavering Farm** **(4)** to another bridge. Keep right on concrete track past barns and out of farmyard. Turn right again along hedge and follow track left between fields, crossing wooded path (an old Roman road).

Follow wide grassy track past low **Roman barrow** **(5)**, winding along edge of field and finally snaking right and left into another field. Follow arrow through gap in hedge and go straight on, with hedge on right, to reach road.

Turn left along road, then right on gravel lane past houses of **Langley Village** **(6)**. At end, just after Boundary House, turn right between hedges and left along fenced tree tunnel. Go on across field towards large oaks and straight on along edge of field.

At junction, turn right along field edge, keeping hedge, and later trees, on right. Follow path round until arrow points right along path through wood. You have, at the grand height of nearly 483ft, reached the **highest point in Essex** **(7)**.

Follow path ahead, with trees on left at first. Walk straight for nearly a mile along grassy path between fields with Chrishall church visible ahead. Turn left and then right round fence of house with pool. Just after barn, join tarmac drive of **Chiswick Hall** **(8)**, leading down to road.

Cross road, turn left and immediately right over footbridge. Walk up path ahead and straight through churchyard of **Holy Trinity** **(9)**. From kissing gate beyond church, go downhill, through another gate and over footbridge.

Cross road and take fenced path through paddock into field. Keep hedge on right and follow path right. Cross lane and keep ahead. Keep hedge (where it exists) on right, following it left. At end, turn right onto Hog's Lane, leading to Red Cow pub in **Chrishall** **(10)**.

LOOK OUT FOR: Newport's **St Mary's church** **(1)** has, among other treasures, a 13th-century portable altar chest with very old oil paintings inside the wooden lid.

Among the streamside, thatched cottages along Hampitt Road in **Arkesden** **(2)** there are at least 15 listed buildings.

Victorian excavations revealed shards of Roman glass and pottery inside the 2nd-century **Roman barrow** **(5)** near **Clavering Farm** **(4)**.

Chrishall's **Holy Trinity church** **(9)** stood in the middle of the medieval village, but is half a mile from today's centre. It dates partly from the 12th century and has 15th-century brasses.

FOOD AND DRINK: The **Axe and Compasses** in Arkesden is a beautiful old pub (www.axeandcompasses.co.uk); the **Red Cow** in Chrishall makes a great endpoint, but is closed from 3pm to 6pm (www.theredcow.com).

TRANSPORT: **Newport** has good local buses and regular trains. **Chrishall** is tricky to get to by public transport, with just an afternoon school bus. A taxi from Audley End station costs about £15. There are occasional buses to and from **Arkesden**. Very energetic walkers might choose to walk all the way from Newport to Meldreth in a day.

Chrishall to Meldreth

8 miles

Ancient ways and flowering fields lead from the quiet village of Chrishall to busier Melbourn and beyond.

Take public footpath opposite Red Cow pub in **Chrishall** **(1)**, straight across playing field and through gap in far hedge. Keep on along path beyond and turn right on lane past thatched cottages. Ignore right turn and look out for the signed Icknield Way Path heading left between houses.

Follow the leafy lane, then fenced path on right of gate to field. Turn left along edge and then right towards trees, still following Icknield Way, passing wood on the left and good views on the right.

A winding, stony track leads out onto road by lily pond. Turn left towards **Heydon** **(2)** beside brick wall. At the little green by Holy Trinity church, turn right onto Fowlmere Road, passing delightful gardens. Opposite Number 76, by a house called 'Woodstock', a wooded grassy path leads left downhill. Go on for a mile through fields bordered by ox-eye daisies, poppies and cornflowers in summer, with wide views ahead.

At a clump of trees, a grassy track – the ancient **Icknield Way** **(3)** itself – crosses the path. Turn left along it for three-quarters of a mile until you reach a lane and turn right, leaving Icknield Way Path. Turn right again along busier road, to emerge onto the A505. Cross over to **Coach House Hotel** **(4)**.

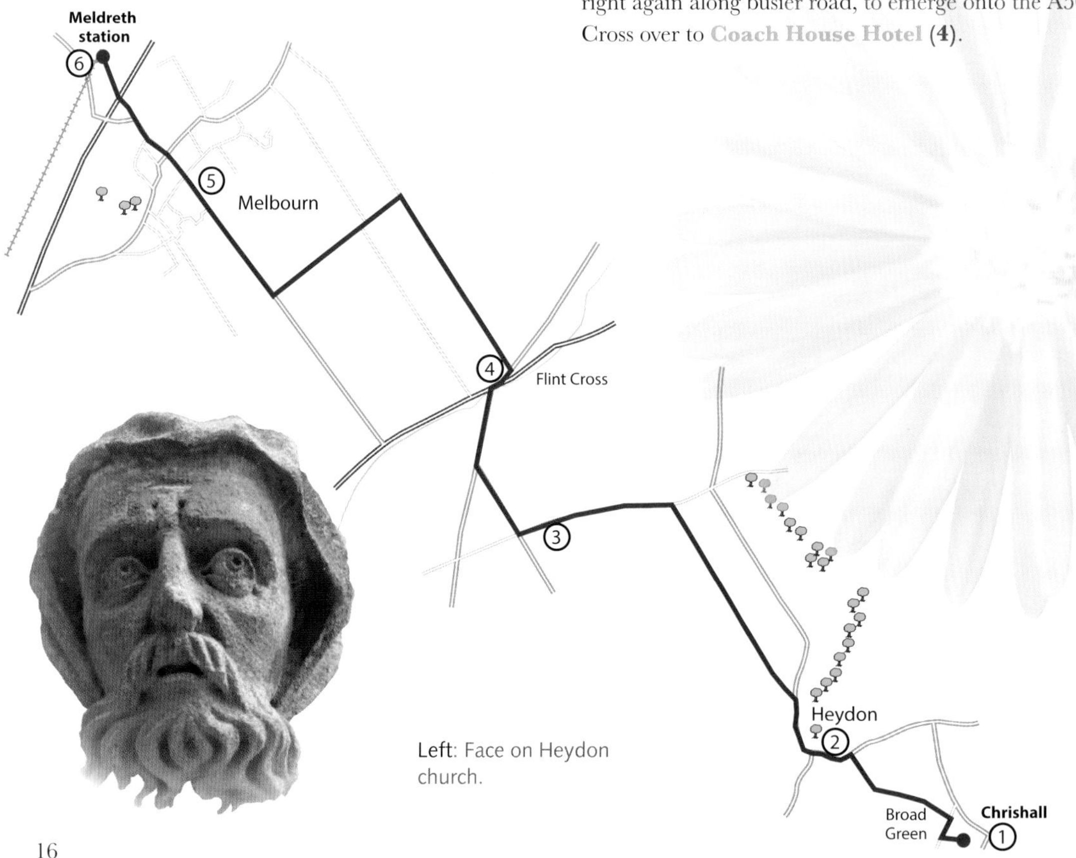

Left: Face on Heydon church.

Above left: Cottage in Heydon.
Above centre: Coach House Hotel, Royston.
Above right: House in Melbourn.

The original Harcamlow route goes left along the main road and right up New Road into Melbourn. But it is far more peaceful to head right to end of Coach House Hotel car park and then left along gravel track leading past Black Peak Farm and over hill. After a mile, just past an overgrown line of trees and bushes on left, double back sharp left to find hidden, grassy track running between hedges to New Road, where you eventually turn right towards **Melbourn** **(5)**.

Simply follow road ahead into the centre of this large village. When you reach High Street, go onto Station Road, passing the church. Cross River Mel near Sheene Mill. Soon after this, a signposted path on right leads under the A10 and over field to **Meldreth** **(6)** station.

LOOK OUT FOR: At nearly 500ft above sea level, **Heydon** **(2)** is one of the highest villages in Cambridgeshire. It is best known locally for Wood Green Animal Shelter's home for rescued small animals.

The **Icknield Way** **(3)**, a pre-Roman route from Dorset to Norfolk, claims to be 'the oldest road in Britain'. Here the Harcamlow joins the Icknield Way Path, marked with axe waymarks, for the second time.

Melbourn **(5)** is a large village with some pretty thatched cottages. Look out for the old Victorian Fire-Engine House at 29 Station Road and 18th-century mill house next to Sheene Mill.

The station lies across a field in the neighbouring village of **Meldreth** **(6)**. A hoard of Bronze Age swords and axes was discovered near the railway station.

FOOD AND DRINK: This walk starts from the lovely **Red Cow** pub in Chrishall. **King William IV** pub is 500m left off the route from Heydon church. After that, **Coach House Hotel** **(4)** (www.coachhousehotel.org.uk), on main road, is the only pub directly on this section and serves drinks and cheap sustaining meals all day. Melbourn, at the end, has several options, from a fish and chip shop (left at the Co-op) to fancy **Sheene Mill** (www.thesheenemill.com).

TRANSPORT: **Chrishall** has very little public transport (see previous walk). **Melbourn**, on the other hand, is well served by buses to Cambridge, and trains from **Meldreth** station leave every hour for Cambridge and London.

Right: Sheene Mill, Melbourn.

Meldreth to Wimpole

9 miles

This cross-country hike ends at Wimpole Hall, set in gently rolling parkland and surrounded by ponds and peaceful woods.

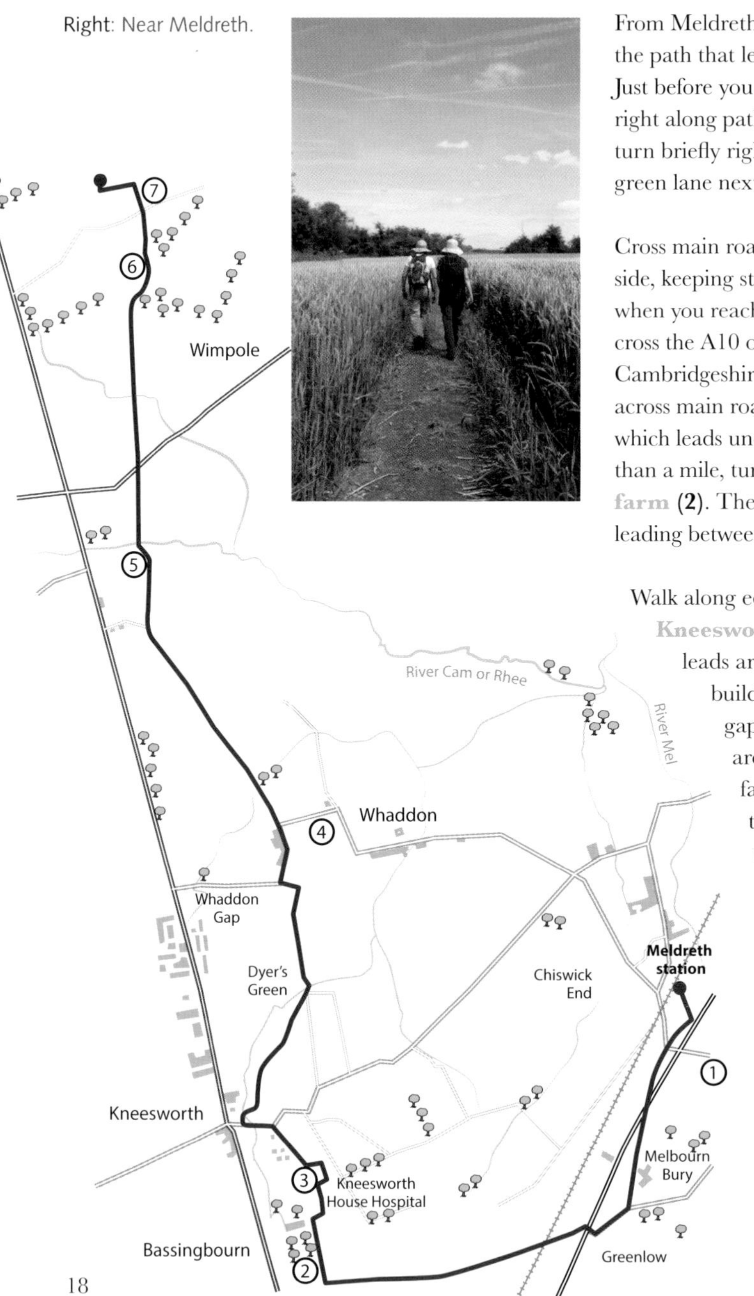

Right: Near Meldreth.

From Meldreth station, walk through fields back along the path that leads towards **Melbourn Village** (**1**). Just before you reach the tunnel under the A10, turn right along path running parallel to it. Cross over and turn briefly right along road at end, then left along green lane next to Fieldgate Nurseries.

Cross main road and turn right along path on far side, keeping straight on past houses. Turn right again when you reach another road. Ignore lane on left and cross the A10 once more to escape at last into quieter Cambridgeshire countryside. Take track, slightly right across main road, signed 'Icknield Way Riders' Route', which leads under the railway. Follow this lane for more than a mile, turning right just before you reach a large **farm** (**2**). There is no waymark, but a clear, grassy path leading between chicken sheds towards trees ahead.

Walk along edge of woods and keep right towards **Kneesworth House Hospital** (**3**). The path leads around right-hand edge of residential buildings. After the last house, head through gap in hedge, turn left and then right around field to emerge by welcoming farm shop. Turn left along road and right through metal kissing gate onto footpath through fields. Keep straight past blue-green reservoir, walking with hedgerow on left to reach crossroads of tracks near a house.

Above left: Kneesworth.
Above centre: Whaddon.
Above right: Wimpole Hall.

Turn left and carry on along sleepy village road. The original Harcamlow route loops right towards Whaddon Green and back, but it is just as pleasant to keep on this lane through the village of Whaddon **(4)**, passing lovely thatched cottages and an old water pump.

Follow road left, then turn right on Church Street, past the green with wooden bus shelter and bench. When road swings right, take path straight on, signed 'To Ermine Street', and follow it for more than a mile. When you reach line of trees, turn left through barrier and then right along path through avenue of lime trees **(5)**. Follow path, curving round overgrown pond, to find brick bridge across little River Cam.

Cross bridge, walk slightly right and then straight along avenue towards distant Wimpole Hall. Cross the A603 and continue in same direction for nearly two miles along a wide, lime-bordered walk. Finally, bear right through a five-barred wooden gate, keeping two 18th-century ponds **(6)**, hidden by clumps of trees, on your left until you reach a gate onto a lane by the stable block of Wimpole Hall **(7)**.

LOOK OUT FOR: Whaddon **(4)** had no electricity or mains water until after the Second World War; local residents used to get their water from a spring beside the road.

An 18th-century landscape gardener called Charles Bridgeman designed the dramatic avenue of lime trees **(5)** that leads to Wimpole Hall. The National Trust now owns the Wimpole estate and there is free public access to everything outside the house and formal gardens. The flowery ditch just before **(6)** is the old ha-ha.

Wimpole's grounds include several ornamental ponds **(6)** and an old stable block, where you can find refreshments and information.

A number of famous architects worked on the mansion at Wimpole Hall **(7)** during the 18th century, including James Gibbs, who also designed Oxford's Radcliffe Camera.

FOOD AND DRINK: There is a farm shop at Fieldgate Nurseries where you can stock up on provisions, and the even more wonderful Hill View Farm Shop near Kneesworth (www.hillviewfarmshop.co.uk). Yuva serves up tasty, Indo-Nepalese meals in Kneesworth's old pub on the main road (www.yuvaroyston.co.uk). The Old Rectory Restaurant, open until 5pm, at Wimpole Hall **(7)** makes a good endpoint and Hardwicke Arms is near the bus stop in Arrington (www.hardwickearms.co.uk).

TRANSPORT: There are regular trains to Meldreth station from Cambridge and London. Three buses per day run to Cambridge from Arrington, the nearest village to Wimpole Hall. On Sundays, 'bike-bus' services go direct from Wimpole Hall (www.scambs.gov.uk/bikebus-explorer).

Right: Village pump in Whaddon.

Wimpole to Cambridge

13 miles

This last walk follows the Wimpole Way back to Cambridge. It is relatively long, but well signposted and easily split into shorter sections.

For a map, download this leaflet: www.visitcambridge.org/dbimgs/WimpoleWay.pdf

Go through gate opposite entrance to stable block at **Wimpole Hall**. Walk past chapel and hall and through another gate. Continue briefly right, bear left up avenue of limes and, at the top, take a sharp right through a third gate along avenue near woods. There are many scenic ways through the Wimpole estate. This is my favourite.

Walk downhill, with trees on left, towards lakes and a gothic folly. Cross Chinese bridge between lakes and turn left by water, then right along edge of fields below folly. Keep going along the field edge and through a gate. At woods cross a bridge and turn right through trees.

Emerging onto road, turn left. Follow Wimpole Way signs left and turn right just after houses. Keep straight along grassy track for nearly two miles. Continue on lane into Kingston. Turn left along The Green and go straight over at crossroads. Don't miss **All Saints and St Andrew** before carrying on out of village.

Turn briefly left onto busier road and then right along Main Street for half a mile, winding over the river towards Caldecote and up past a church and farmhouses. Just before phone box, turn right on footpath and left at first field boundary, soon walking along edge of **Hardwick Wood**, still following Wimpole Way signs.

Finally, at a post with arrows, turn right across fields towards Hardwick. After nearly a mile, turn left onto Hardwick's Main Street and right after a few steps. (The village itself, with pub, shop and buses, is straight ahead.)

Follow grassy path as it continues between hedges. Turn left in trees, then right, following Wimpole Way arrows, along field edge with view ahead of still-distant Cambridge. Continue for half a mile to road. Without crossing, turn left on grassy track, parallel to road, over wooden footbridge and on up path beside paddock. Turn right across road and follow path ahead through small wood and Barton Road Rifle Range. Where path ends, follow lane through **Coton**, past St Peter's church.

Turn right at junction beyond church onto winding road leading to Plough Inn. Go straight on beyond pub on lane called 'The Footpath', which becomes a track between trees leading to a bridge over the M11. Keep following Wimpole Way on far side (watch out for bikes!). Follow tarmac path left, then right, passing buildings

Below left: Kingston church.
Below centre: Devil in Kingston church.
Below right: Lake at Wimpole Hall.

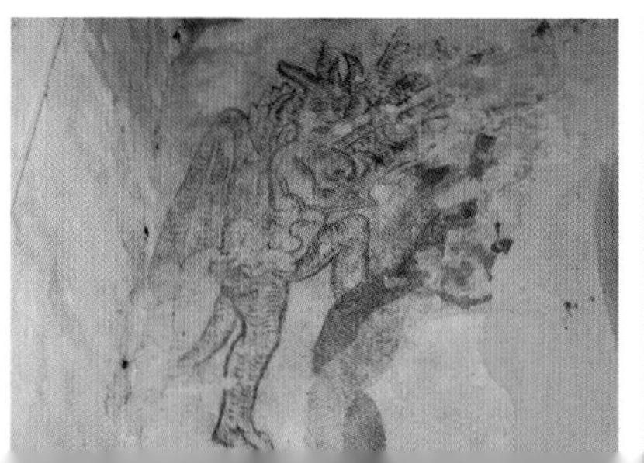